The library of
Stable Management

Choosing and buying your horse

**Mark Hallion
and Julie Langrish**

The library of Stable Management

Choosing and Buying your horse

Contents

The authors would like to thank the following for their help:
- Malcolm Dunning Saddlery
- Jeremy Mantell MRCVS
- Mrs. Gillian Knight and Mrs. Yvonne Bryant for modelling

Chapter One

Introduction

The horse has evolved over 60 million years and has been domesticated for under 5,000 years. The common practice of stabling horses has occurred only during the last 500 years. During the last 100 years, technology has relieved the horse of its key role in civilisation as cars and planes have removed it as a form of transport.

A minority of people have never considered the possibility of a world without horses. Hunting, racing, show jumping and the fast-growing discipline of dressage have always had their followings. All these aspects of the horse world continue to grow in popularity. More and more people are taking to the saddle. Television has introduced the glamour of the horse world to our homes. The excitement of a top show jumper going against the clock to win

Gill Knight under instruction at Mayhill Stud.

four to six weeks. You will have to pay more if you want stud holes or road nails.

If you own somewhere where you can keep your pony or horse, then that is ideal but remember you need at least three acres so that you can rest the fields alternately.

Livery yards, providing they are good, are most generally used and, if you are working full time, they save you the worry of having to leave your horse unattended for most of the day. Full livery means that you pay for stabling, bedding, feeding, watering and grooming, and the horse being turned out for exercise. Part or working livery stables are usually run by riding stables, and the horse is cared for at a reduced fee in return for its use by the school. A riding school has to be licensed, so make sure that your chosen stables is covered.

Many people keep their horses at DIY yards where stabling, feed and bedding are available for a fee, but you look after your own horse. Again, providing the place is good, this establishment can be ideal. Beware of any yard where all the horses are turned out together in fields surrounded with barbed wire fencing, and which have inexperienced people in charge. Prices vary greatly at these yards and some have very peculiar rules and regulations, so tread carefully.

The Authors' own yard - Mayhill Stud.

Chapter Three

Which horse is right for you?

The number one consideration is how experienced you are. This book is aimed at the novice rider and the first-time buyer – a very vulnerable person. Your greatest asset is knowing and having help from an experienced, knowledgeable person whom you can trust. It is this person who, hopefully, will help you find your horse and also who can save you a lot of hassle and heartbreak later on if you get the wrong one.

You need to consider many things in your choice of a horse. What do you want it to do? Do you want it just to hack or do you want to further your own riding education and find a horse that is going to help you? Are you looking for a 'schoolmaster' type that can jump safely and perhaps has some dressage experience? Do you want to hunt?

Your first horse may not be the one you will keep forever. At this moment you may not have any long-term ideas apart from simply being a horse owner and gaining more knowledge and experience. Therefore, the horse you buy must be suitable for the job you require of it.

Let us start with size. You have to feel comfortable with the height and build of the

A schoolmaster in action.

like appearance. These are less likely to absorb concussion and horses with such feet may suffer more from lameness.

After this initial examination, ask for the horse to be paraded in front of you, first at walk and then at trot. Any lameness at this point will be detected by the horse's movement. Any out-of-sequence steps, the head dropping or the quarters rising uncharacteristically, point to lameness. If all is well, check the horse's action to see if it moves straight. Stand in front of the horse and have it trotted towards you. Check to see if its legs swing out, an action known as 'dishing' or 'plaiting'. Although moving straight is important for dressage and showing, it is not crucial for other aspects of the sport.

The next step is to see the horse ridden. Never attempt to ride it without seeing it being ridden by someone else first. Pay particular heed to the tack that is used. A very strong bit and standing martingale, for example, usually indicate that the horse is strong and moves with an excessively high head carriage.

While the horse is being ridden, make sure it is worked around you, close enough so that you can pay particular attention to its action. A rider's weight often shows up a lameness that was not previously visible. Study the horse at all its different paces: walk, trot, canter and gallop. Check for its willingness to comply with the rider's aids. Once the horse has cantered, ask to see it cantered in a small area. If it is able to sustain its canter you will have a good indication of how well balanced it is.

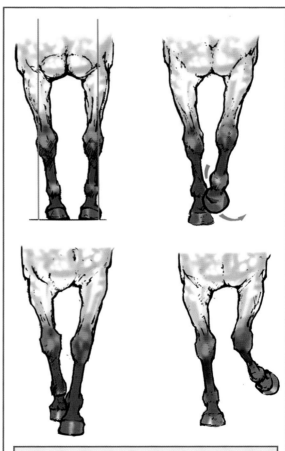

Top left: Crooked in front. Top right: Brushing. Bottom left: Plaiting. Bottom right: Dishing.

After a successful trial and veterinary inspection, your new purchase is ready to go home.

Pay particular attention to the horse's breathing. A roaring, rather than rasping, breathing sound indicates a horse with wind problems. It is unlikely that such an animal could participate in anything too strenuous and perhaps you should avoid it.

Whether or not you are interested in jumping, it is a good idea to see the horse jump. Apart from the opportunity to see its capabilities as a jumper, it enables the horse to demonstrate its willingness to please.

Ask to see the horse ridden along the road so you can check its behaviour in traffic. This also provides the opportunity to see if it is willing to leave the stable yard or field and not be nappy.

Having seen the horse ridden, you may now decide to have a go yourself. Always wear suitable riding clothes and a hard hat.

When you first climb aboard a new horse, do not rush, allow time to familiarise yourself with it. Walk around for a few minutes. If the horse is in a dealer's yard, it may have had several riders on its back recently and will need time to familiarise itself with you as well. When you feel comfortable, progress gradually through the horse's paces. Some yards may have an indoor school and this is the ideal place to ride first, especially if you are very inexperienced.

However you try the horse, be sure to

ask it to do different things than the rider who showed it to you. It is very likely that the horse will have been shown to you doing the things it likes best and in a way that it prefers. After all, it is being sold and it is unlikely that it will be asked to do something that shows it in a bad light.

Once you are happy with the horse, you might like to try a jump or take it into a larger field. Never attempt to do either of these things unless you are totally happy that you are in control and are confident in your mount.

If all goes well, you may decide there and then that this is the horse for you. If you are uncertain, do not worry about asking to go back and try it again or to take someone experienced back with you.

If this is the horse you want to buy, you now need to agree the purchase price and arrange for the vetting. As a precautionary measure, pay a small deposit which is refunded if the horse fails the vet, or deducted from the purchase price on completion of the successful vetting.

Some people go to the trouble and expense of having a horse vetted and, even if it passes with flying colours, do not go on to buy it. Generally speaking, if you agree to buy a horse subject to vet and it passes, you should buy it.

We strongly advise you to agree a price before the vetting so that everything is clear at this point. Usually, the vendor likes you to pay for and collect the horse as soon as possible and we feel that you should do this without delay because you never know what may happen once you have paid for it and left it for a week.

A cheque has to clear, so a banker's draft is a good method of payment and means that you can take your horse home straight away. A caring owner should give you a list of what feed the horse has been having so that there is no drastic change of diet, the date when it was last wormed and with what, possibly when it was last shod and, hopefully, an up-to-date tetanus and influenza certificate. If this latter has been neglected, then it is advisable to start a new course as soon as possible and also have the horse's teeth checked and rasped if necessary.

The young horse

For your first horse, a young, unbroken animal is not advisable but, as we said earlier, if you have consistent expert help and it is your dream to do the whole thing yourself, it may be done.

Depending on your riding and handling experience, you have to be prepared for your experienced trainer to do 99 per cent of the training for you, even though you should remain consistently involved. Backing the young horse is a deep and complex experience, but highly enjoyable and fulfilling.

Chapter Five

The veterinary inspection

**J A R Mantell, MRCVS
The Equine
Veterinary Hospital,
Liphook, Hampshire,
England.**

The purchase of any horse involves the taking of a risk; no horse is risk free and the best the veterinary surgeon can do is to try to identify, assess and quantify that risk for you, the buyer, before you decide whether or not to proceed with the purchase.

By the time of the pre-purchase examination, you will have already chosen that particular horse. In other words, you have considered such things as colour, height, type and suitability for the task. If in doubt, consult your trainers before this stage.

Choose a veterinary surgeon either known or recommended to you. If that is not possible, ask your own veterinary surgeon to recommend a vet in the area in which the horse is. Ensure that you talk with the vet to discuss your requirements before the examination, or be present at the time. The choice of vet is a personal one but as a general rule it is better to instruct an experienced equine vet who may also be a horseman, rather than a horseman who may also be a vet.

Types of examination

There is only one type of pre-purchase veterinary examination. All the rest are cheap imitations and you should not and cannot expect to get the same opinion for a considerably lower fee. If you want to be protected when purchasing a horse by obtaining a professional opinion and if you wish to have a form of certificate that is

Checking heart and respiration.

**Testing the front for bruising
or internal damage.**

acceptable to insurance companies, then a full 5-stage vetting is the only option. All other types, commonly known as 'insurance vettings', 'heart, eyes and lungs', 'running an eye over' and a 'quick vetting' are cheaper, and thus poorer, imitations. Despite ill-informed legal opinion, they do not give you any form of protection.

The 5-stage vetting has evolved over decades and its aim is to achieve a cost-effective evaluation and assessment of a particular horse's suitability to perform a certain task. It is an examination carried out on a given day and the opinion relates to that day; no long-term warranty or guarantee of health can be expected, although obviously the examining vet will try to advise you about the long-term implications of any abnormalities detected.

Horses are no longer classified as 'sound' or 'unsound', nor should they 'pass' or 'fail' a vetting. The opinion given nowadays, sadly enforced upon us by the increasingly litigious nature of society, is that 'the effects noted above are/are not likely to prejudice this animal's use for ...'

The examination

Unless the opinion is to be compromised, there are certain basic requirements for the environment in which a vetting takes place. These are:

1. A dark stable in which to examine the eyes.
2. An area of hard level ground, preferably concrete or tarmac, on which the horse may be walked and trotted in-hand.
3. An area in which the horse may be ridden safely, including the ability to canter hard or gallop as required.
4. In addition, the ability to lunge or trot on a hard circle may also be of considerable benefit.

If the vendor does not have such facilities, consider moving the examination to a different location. The actual examination usually takes place in a set routine according to personal choice and includes the following stages:

1. Initial examination in a stable.
   Observe in stable. Heart and lungs.
   Eyes. Examination of head, teeth,

throat, and so on. General assessment of type and condition.

2. Outside in daylight to observe the whole horse when standing square. Then walk and trot in hand in a straight line. Turning and backing. Probably flexion tests. Possibly lunging or trotting in a circle.

3. Examination under saddle. This includes mounting, walking, trotting, cantering and probably galloping depending on the type and fitness of the horse. This exercise should be both in circles and in more extended straight lines.

4. Whilst the horse cools down from exercise, the vet makes a more thorough and detailed examination of its hooves, limbs and body, noting and assessing any abnormalities. The formal identification will probably take place now.

5. Once the heart rate has returned to normal, the vet (a) performs the final trot up which may also include further turning, circling and flexion tests and

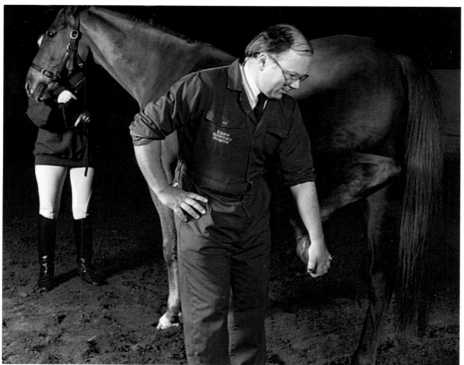

Hind flexion test.

Front flexion test.

25

(b) takes the blood sample for medication analysis.

6. Finally, the vet will discuss with you the findings of the examination and produce a written report.

Limitations and extra tests

There is also a pre-purchase examination, which is a clinical examination and does not involve laboratory or diagnostic techniques. It does not, unless specifically requested, include any examination for pregnancy. The ageing of horses is notoriously inaccurate and comprehensive research over the last few years has indicated that the previously-accepted methods of aging by dentition can be wildly inaccurate, even in very experienced hands. Thus, it should be accepted that it is not possible to age a horse accurately by looking at its dentition. So it is vital that, if possible, documentary evidence of the age be obtained prior to purchase.

Radiographs are not necessarily the black and white answers that everybody hopes for. Indeed, they may even complicate rather than clarify the issue. It is my opinion that, unless specifically requested either by an insurance company or by the purchaser, the decision whether or not to X-ray should be left to the examining vet based on his clinical findings at the time of the examination. Routine pre-purchase X-rays are not nearly as helpful as is sometimes expected.

Similar arguments may also be made for routine tendon scanning. Endoscopy of the upper airway may be a more useful technique but again it should be discussed prior to the examination so that the purchaser is aware of the limitations.

It is not normal to carry out routine haematological blood testing but, if this is required, a sample should be taken before, not after, exercise.

Blood testing for the presence of medication likely to affect the results of the examination is extremely worthwhile, both from the vendor's and purchaser's point of view. There are various methods for taking and storing this sample but, if nothing else, it certainly appears to work as a deterrent if the vendor knows that a sample will be taken!

Warranties

Warranties are a matter between the vendor and the purchaser. Under the Trades Descriptions Acts, purchasers are advised to obtain a warranty from the vendor stating that the horse or pony is or is not free from vices, allergies and so on. A warranty that it is safe to shoe, load and be ridden in traffic may also be useful. Exact heights are a matter between vendor and purchaser and are not part of the vetting examination. The only form of certification for exact height measurements is the JMB certificate. It is worth enquiring about the horse's previous medical history and also for a simple

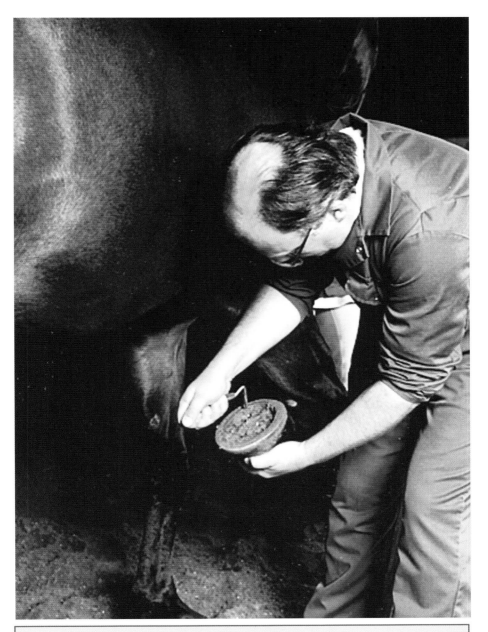

Examining the feet.

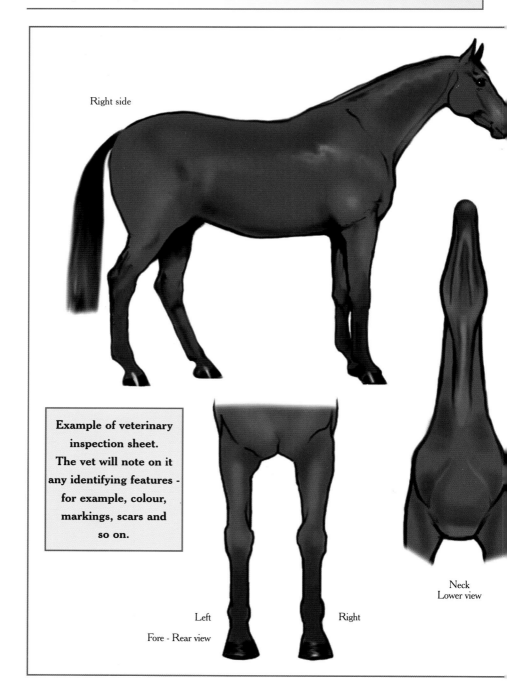

Right side

Example of veterinary
inspection sheet.
The vet will note on it
any identifying features -
for example, colour,
markings, scars and
so on.

Left

Right

Fore - Rear view

Neck
Lower view

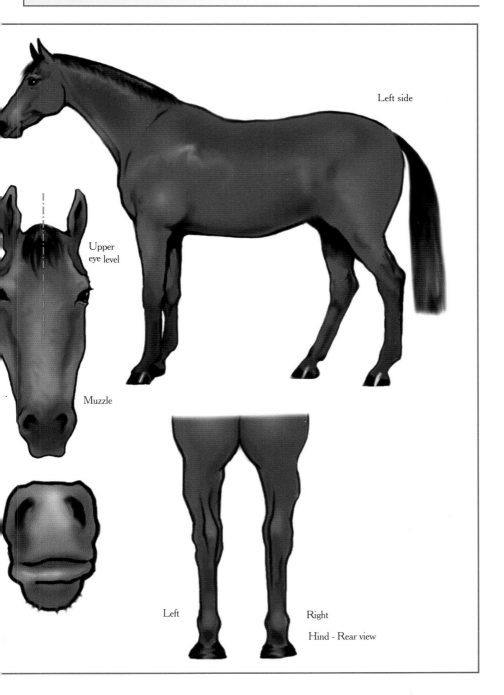

Left side

Upper
eye level

Muzzle

Left   Right

Hind - Rear view

statement from the vendor to confirm that this horse has not received any medication likely to affect the results of the examination.

After thoughts

The pre-purchase veterinary examination is continuing to change and respond to the requirements, not only of the potential purchasers but also the requirements of the legal profession. Increasing consumer legislation and the litigious nature of society unfortunately has meant that the opinion is now more likely to be given under legal restraints rather than be the old-fashioned personal opinion of an experienced vet.

Communication is the key between vet and purchaser so that both sides know the intentions and limitations of the examination. The move towards the continental system of a comprehensive check list which details the findings but gives no opinion as to suitability may be a natural development, but personally I believe that most purchasers really want to obtain an experienced opinion assessing the risks and suitability of that horse for the purpose. It cannot be over-emphasised that thorough communication between purchaser and vet is the key to success.

Do be aware that a vetting is not the same as an insurance examination. It is quite possible to 'pass' a vetting yet later find that insurance proves difficult because of the findings. The vetting assesses the horse's suitability for the purchaser's intended use, whilst the insurance companies are interested in making exclusions on any abnormality. It is always wise to obtain insurance cover before purchase, not afterwards.

The pre-purchase examination of a horse has stood the test of time and continues to offer a prospective purchaser a cost-effective way of assessing a horse's suitability for a specific use. Having a horse 'vetted' before purchase should, hopefully, lessen the risk of buying one that needs extensive treatment afterwards.

Glossary

Bog spavin - A swelling of the front of the hock area

Clipping - The removal of a horse's winter coat

Conformation - The physical make-up of the horse

Crib biting - The chewing of wood, usually that of the stable door or inside the stable, most often due to boredom

Ewe neck - A neck which curves upwards

Mareish - A term used to describe a mare in season. A time in which they can become sensitive, highly strung and, sometimes, aggressive

Nappy - Not willing to respond to a rider's aids or wishes. The horse may refuse to go forward or may even try to go in the opposite direction

Road nails - Nails with tungsten grips to assist grip on slippery surfaces

Sound in wind - A term which describes the healthy condition of a horse's lungs (breathing)

Standing martingale - A leather strap which runs from the girth to the noseband via a neck strap

Stud holes - Holes in the horse's shoes prepared with threads for the insertion of metal studs

Thorough pin - An egg shaped swelling on the side of the hock

Weaving - A condition where the horse stands and swings his head from side to side, usually when in his stable

Wind sucking - A condition where a horse will grab hold of the top of a stable door or any similar surface, tense his muscles and appear to suck in air

Index